W9-CDI-192

KEVIN HARVICK

Nicole Pristash

PowerKiDS press™

New York

Published in 2009 by The Rosen Publishing Group, Inc.
29 East 21st Street, New York, NY 10010

First Edition

Book Design: Michael J. Flynn
Layout Design: Kate Laczynski
Photo Researcher: Jessica Gerweck

Photo Credits: All images © Getty Images, Inc.

Library of Congress Cataloging-in-Publication Data

Pristash, Nicole.
   Kevin Harvick / Nicole Pristash. — 1st ed.
      p. cm. — (NASCAR champions)
   Includes index.
   ISBN 978-1-4042-4448-1 (library binding) ISBN 978-1-4042-4544-0 (pbk)
   ISBN 978-1-4042-4562-4 (6-pack)
   1. Harvick, Kevin—Juvenile literature. 2. Automobile racing drivers—United States—Biography—Juvenile literature. I. Title. II. Series.
   GV1032.H357P75 2009
   796.72092—dc22
   [B]
                                             2007047424

Manufactured in the United States of America

"NASCAR" is a registered trademark of the National Association for Stock Car Auto Racing, Inc.

Contents

Kevin Harvick is a race car driver. He drives for NASCAR. He was born in Bakersfield, California.

4

When Kevin was young, his family gave him a go-kart, or small race car. He then decided to become a race car driver.

Kevin started by racing trucks. He entered the Craftsman Truck **Series** in 1995. He learned a lot about racing.

8

The Childress Racing team liked Kevin's racing **skills**. They asked Kevin to **join** their team.

10

11

Kevin quickly became a winner. He won five races his first year in the Busch Series! The next step was the Winston Cup.

13

Kevin was in a car **crash** in 2002 during a Winston Cup race, in North Carolina. He was not hurt, though.

In 2003, Kevin won the Brickyard 400. Kevin and his team kissed the **bricks** at the start and finish line. This is a NASCAR **tradition**.

16

In 2006, Kevin won his second Busch Series **championship**. It was a great moment for him.

18

Kevin Harvick is quickly becoming one of NASCAR's top drivers. He hopes to get even better and to stay a **champion**.

20

Glossary

bricks (BRIKS) Blocks of baked clay used for building.

champion (CHAM-pee-un) The best, or the winner.

championship (CHAM-pee-un-ship) A race held to decide the best, or the winner.

crash (KRASH) To have run into something hard.

join (JOYN) To come together or take part in.

series (SIR-eez) A group of races.

skills (SKILZ) Abilities to do things well.

tradition (truh-DIH-shun) A way of doing something that has been passed down over time.

22

Books and Web Sites

Books

Doeden, Matt. *NASCAR: Behind the Scenes*. Blazers, 2008.

Kelley, K.C. *NASCAR: Authorized Handbook*. Pleasantville, NY: Reader's Digest, 2005.

Web Sites

Due to the changing nature of Internet links, the Rosen Publishing Group, Inc., has developed an online list of Web sites related to the subject of this book. This site is updated regularly. Please use this link to access the list: www.powerkidslinks.com/nascar/harvick/

23

Index